50 Farmhouse Kitchen Recipes for Home

By: Kelly Johnson

Table of Contents

- Buttermilk Biscuits
- Southern Fried Chicken
- Cornbread
- Chicken Pot Pie
- Beef Stew
- Apple Pie
- Country Fried Steak
- Fried Green Tomatoes
- Macaroni and Cheese
- Corn Chowder
- Meatloaf
- Deviled Eggs
- Farmhouse Salad with Homemade Dressing
- Sourdough Bread
- Chicken and Dumplings
- Pulled Pork Sandwiches
- Collard Greens
- Baked Beans
- Pumpkin Pie
- Chicken Casserole
- Tomato Soup
- Cornbread Stuffing
- Blackberry Cobbler
- Mashed Potatoes
- Beef Pot Roast
- Fried Catfish
- Green Bean Casserole
- Potato Salad
- Banana Bread
- Ham and Bean Soup
- Fried Chicken Livers
- Corn Pudding
- Lemonade
- Apple Crisp
- Shepherd's Pie

- Cabbage Rolls
- Pickled Beets
- Grits
- Biscuits and Gravy
- Chicken Fried Rice
- Peach Cobbler
- Corn Fritters
- Baked Macaroni and Cheese
- Coleslaw
- Lemon Bars
- Strawberry Jam
- BBQ Ribs
- Farmhouse Omelette
- Chocolate Chip Cookies
- Farmhouse Breakfast Hash

Buttermilk Biscuits

Ingredients:

- 2 cups all-purpose flour
- 1 tablespoon baking powder
- 1/2 teaspoon baking soda
- 1/2 teaspoon salt
- 6 tablespoons cold unsalted butter, cut into small cubes
- 3/4 cup cold buttermilk

Instructions:

1. Preheat your oven to 450°F (230°C). Line a baking sheet with parchment paper or lightly grease it.
2. In a large mixing bowl, whisk together the flour, baking powder, baking soda, and salt until well combined.
3. Add the cold butter cubes to the dry ingredients. Using a pastry cutter or your fingers, cut the butter into the flour mixture until it resembles coarse crumbs with some larger pea-sized pieces of butter remaining.
4. Make a well in the center of the flour mixture and pour in the cold buttermilk. Stir with a fork or spatula until the dough comes together. It will be slightly sticky.
5. Turn the dough out onto a lightly floured surface. Gently knead it a few times until it holds together, but be careful not to overwork the dough.
6. Pat the dough into a rectangle about 3/4 inch (2 cm) thick. Use a floured biscuit cutter or a glass to cut out biscuits, pressing straight down without twisting the cutter. Place the biscuits on the prepared baking sheet, leaving a little space between each one.
7. Gather any scraps of dough, gently pat them together, and cut out more biscuits until all the dough is used.
8. Bake the biscuits in the preheated oven for 10-12 minutes, or until they are golden brown on top and cooked through.
9. Remove the biscuits from the oven and serve warm. Enjoy them with butter, jam, honey, or as a side to your favorite meals.

Southern Fried Chicken

Ingredients:

- 1 whole chicken, cut into pieces (or use your preferred chicken parts)
- 2 cups buttermilk
- 2 cups all-purpose flour
- 2 teaspoons salt
- 1 teaspoon black pepper
- 1 teaspoon paprika
- 1 teaspoon garlic powder
- 1 teaspoon onion powder
- 1/2 teaspoon cayenne pepper (adjust according to your spice preference)
- Vegetable oil, for frying

Instructions:

1. In a large bowl, place the chicken pieces and cover them with buttermilk. Let them soak for at least 1 hour or overnight in the refrigerator. This helps tenderize the chicken and adds flavor.
2. In another bowl, mix together the flour, salt, black pepper, paprika, garlic powder, onion powder, and cayenne pepper to make the seasoned flour mixture.
3. Heat vegetable oil in a large skillet or deep fryer to 350°F (175°C).
4. Remove the chicken pieces from the buttermilk, allowing any excess to drip off.
5. Dredge each piece of chicken in the seasoned flour mixture, coating it thoroughly. Shake off any excess flour.
6. Carefully place the chicken pieces into the hot oil, making sure not to overcrowd the pan. Fry in batches if necessary.
7. Fry the chicken for about 15-20 minutes, turning occasionally, until golden brown and cooked through. The internal temperature should reach 165°F (75°C).
8. Once the chicken is cooked, remove it from the oil and place it on a wire rack or paper towels to drain excess oil.
9. Serve the Southern Fried Chicken hot, accompanied by your favorite sides such as mashed potatoes, coleslaw, biscuits, or gravy. Enjoy the crispy and flavorful goodness!

Cornbread

Ingredients:

- 1 cup yellow cornmeal
- 1 cup all-purpose flour
- 1/4 cup granulated sugar (optional, adjust to taste)
- 1 tablespoon baking powder
- 1 teaspoon salt
- 1 cup buttermilk
- 1/2 cup unsalted butter, melted (plus extra for greasing the pan)
- 2 large eggs

Instructions:

1. Preheat your oven to 400°F (200°C). Grease a 9-inch cast iron skillet or baking dish with butter.
2. In a large mixing bowl, combine the cornmeal, flour, sugar (if using), baking powder, and salt. Stir until well combined.
3. In a separate bowl, whisk together the buttermilk, melted butter, and eggs until smooth.
4. Pour the wet ingredients into the dry ingredients and stir until just combined. Be careful not to overmix; a few lumps are okay.
5. Pour the batter into the prepared skillet or baking dish, spreading it out evenly.
6. Bake in the preheated oven for 20-25 minutes, or until the cornbread is golden brown on top and a toothpick inserted into the center comes out clean.
7. Remove the cornbread from the oven and let it cool in the skillet or baking dish for a few minutes before slicing and serving.
8. Serve the cornbread warm as a side dish with butter, honey, or your favorite chili or stew. Enjoy the moist and flavorful Southern cornbread!

Chicken Pot Pie

Ingredients:

For the filling:

- 2 tablespoons unsalted butter
- 1 onion, chopped
- 2 carrots, peeled and diced
- 2 celery stalks, diced
- 2 cloves garlic, minced
- 1/4 cup all-purpose flour
- 2 cups chicken broth
- 1 cup milk
- 2 cups cooked chicken, shredded or diced
- 1 cup frozen peas
- 1 teaspoon dried thyme
- Salt and pepper to taste

For the crust:

- 1 package (2 sheets) store-bought puff pastry or pie crust

Instructions:

1. Preheat your oven to 400°F (200°C).
2. In a large skillet or pot, melt the butter over medium heat. Add the chopped onion, carrots, celery, and garlic. Cook, stirring occasionally, until the vegetables are softened, about 5-7 minutes.
3. Sprinkle the flour over the cooked vegetables and stir to combine. Cook for an additional 1-2 minutes to cook off the raw flour taste.
4. Gradually pour in the chicken broth and milk, stirring constantly to prevent lumps from forming. Bring the mixture to a simmer and cook until thickened, about 5 minutes.
5. Stir in the cooked chicken, frozen peas, dried thyme, salt, and pepper. Taste and adjust seasoning as needed. Remove the skillet from the heat.

6. Roll out the puff pastry or pie crust on a lightly floured surface to fit the size of your baking dish.
7. Pour the chicken mixture into a 9-inch pie dish or similar-sized baking dish.
8. Carefully place the rolled-out pastry dough over the top of the filling, pressing the edges to seal. If using puff pastry, you can make a few slits in the pastry to allow steam to escape.
9. Place the pie dish on a baking sheet (to catch any drips) and bake in the preheated oven for 25-30 minutes, or until the crust is golden brown and the filling is bubbling.
10. Remove the chicken pot pie from the oven and let it cool for a few minutes before serving. Enjoy the comforting flavors of this classic dish!

Beef Stew

Ingredients:

- 2 pounds stew beef, cut into 1-inch cubes
- 1/4 cup all-purpose flour
- Salt and pepper to taste
- 2 tablespoons olive oil
- 1 large onion, chopped
- 3 cloves garlic, minced
- 4 cups beef broth
- 1 cup red wine (optional)
- 2 bay leaves
- 1 teaspoon dried thyme
- 1 teaspoon dried rosemary
- 4 carrots, peeled and sliced
- 4 potatoes, peeled and cubed
- 2 stalks celery, chopped
- 1 cup frozen peas (optional)
- Chopped fresh parsley for garnish (optional)

Instructions:

1. In a large bowl, combine the cubed stew beef with the flour, salt, and pepper, tossing to coat the beef evenly.
2. Heat the olive oil in a large pot or Dutch oven over medium-high heat. Add the coated beef cubes in batches and brown them on all sides. Remove the browned beef from the pot and set aside.
3. In the same pot, add the chopped onion and garlic. Cook, stirring occasionally, until the onion is softened and translucent, about 5 minutes.
4. Return the browned beef cubes to the pot. Pour in the beef broth and red wine (if using), scraping the bottom of the pot to release any browned bits.
5. Stir in the bay leaves, dried thyme, and dried rosemary. Bring the mixture to a simmer, then reduce the heat to low. Cover and let the stew simmer for about 1.5 to 2 hours, or until the beef is tender.
6. Add the sliced carrots, cubed potatoes, and chopped celery to the pot. Continue to simmer, covered, for an additional 30 minutes, or until the vegetables are tender.

7. If using frozen peas, add them to the stew during the last 5 minutes of cooking.
8. Taste the stew and adjust the seasoning with salt and pepper if needed.
9. Remove the bay leaves from the stew before serving. Ladle the beef stew into bowls and garnish with chopped fresh parsley if desired.
10. Serve the beef stew hot, with crusty bread or biscuits on the side. Enjoy the comforting flavors of this classic dish!

Apple Pie

Ingredients:

For the crust:

- 2 1/2 cups all-purpose flour
- 1 teaspoon salt
- 1 tablespoon granulated sugar
- 1 cup unsalted butter, cold and cut into small pieces
- 6-8 tablespoons ice water

For the filling:

- 6-7 large apples (such as Granny Smith or Honeycrisp), peeled, cored, and thinly sliced
- 1/2 cup granulated sugar
- 1/4 cup packed brown sugar
- 2 tablespoons all-purpose flour
- 1 teaspoon ground cinnamon
- 1/4 teaspoon ground nutmeg
- 1 tablespoon lemon juice
- 1 tablespoon unsalted butter, cut into small pieces

For assembly:

- 1 egg, beaten (for egg wash)
- 1 tablespoon granulated sugar (for sprinkling)

Instructions:

1. Prepare the crust: In a large mixing bowl, combine the flour, salt, and sugar. Add the cold butter pieces and use a pastry cutter or your fingers to cut the butter into the flour mixture until it resembles coarse crumbs with some pea-sized pieces of butter remaining.
2. Gradually add the ice water, 1 tablespoon at a time, and mix until the dough just begins to come together. Be careful not to overwork the dough. Divide the dough in half, shape each half into a disc, and wrap them tightly in plastic wrap. Refrigerate the dough for at least 1 hour before using.
3. Preheat your oven to 375°F (190°C). Place a baking sheet in the oven to preheat.

4. Prepare the filling: In a large bowl, combine the sliced apples, granulated sugar, brown sugar, flour, cinnamon, nutmeg, and lemon juice. Toss until the apples are evenly coated.
5. Roll out one disc of chilled dough on a lightly floured surface into a circle large enough to fit into a 9-inch pie dish with some overhang. Carefully transfer the dough to the pie dish and gently press it into the bottom and sides.
6. Pour the apple filling into the prepared pie crust, mounding it slightly in the center. Dot the top of the filling with small pieces of butter.
7. Roll out the second disc of chilled dough and place it over the filling. Trim any excess dough and crimp the edges to seal. Cut a few slits in the top crust to allow steam to escape.
8. Brush the top crust with beaten egg and sprinkle with granulated sugar for a golden finish.
9. Place the pie on the preheated baking sheet and bake in the preheated oven for 50-60 minutes, or until the crust is golden brown and the filling is bubbly.
10. Allow the pie to cool for at least 2 hours before slicing and serving. Serve warm or at room temperature, optionally with a scoop of vanilla ice cream or a dollop of whipped cream. Enjoy the delicious homemade apple pie!

Country Fried Steak

Ingredients:

For the steak:

- 4 cube steaks (about 4 ounces each), tenderized
- Salt and pepper to taste
- 1 cup all-purpose flour
- 1 teaspoon garlic powder
- 1 teaspoon paprika
- 1/2 teaspoon onion powder
- 1/4 teaspoon cayenne pepper (optional)
- 2 eggs
- 1/4 cup milk
- Vegetable oil, for frying

For the gravy:

- 1/4 cup all-purpose flour
- 2 cups milk
- Salt and pepper to taste

Instructions:

1. Season the cube steaks generously with salt and pepper on both sides.
2. In a shallow dish, combine the flour, garlic powder, paprika, onion powder, and cayenne pepper (if using).
3. In another shallow dish, whisk together the eggs and milk.
4. Dredge each cube steak in the seasoned flour, shaking off any excess. Dip the floured steaks into the egg mixture, then dredge them again in the flour mixture, pressing gently to adhere.
5. Heat vegetable oil in a large skillet over medium heat. Add enough oil to cover the bottom of the skillet by about 1/4 inch.
6. Carefully place the breaded cube steaks in the hot oil. Cook for 3-4 minutes on each side, or until golden brown and crispy. Depending on the size of your skillet, you may need to cook the steaks in batches to avoid overcrowding.

7. Once the steaks are cooked, transfer them to a paper towel-lined plate to drain excess oil.
8. To make the gravy, pour off all but about 2 tablespoons of the oil from the skillet. Sprinkle the flour over the remaining oil and whisk to combine, scraping up any browned bits from the bottom of the skillet.
9. Gradually pour in the milk, whisking constantly to prevent lumps from forming. Cook the gravy over medium heat, stirring frequently, until it thickens to your desired consistency. Season with salt and pepper to taste.
10. Serve the country fried steaks hot, topped with the creamy gravy. Enjoy this classic Southern comfort food with mashed potatoes, green beans, or your favorite side dishes!

Fried Green Tomatoes

Ingredients:

- 4 green tomatoes, sliced into 1/4-inch rounds
- Salt and pepper to taste
- 1/2 cup all-purpose flour
- 2 large eggs
- 1 tablespoon milk
- 1 cup cornmeal or breadcrumbs
- 1/2 teaspoon paprika (optional)
- Vegetable oil, for frying

Instructions:

1. Place the sliced green tomatoes on a paper towel-lined baking sheet. Sprinkle them with salt and pepper on both sides and let them sit for about 10-15 minutes. This helps draw out excess moisture from the tomatoes.
2. In three separate shallow dishes, prepare the breading station: one with flour, one with beaten eggs mixed with milk, and one with cornmeal or breadcrumbs mixed with paprika (if using).
3. Heat vegetable oil in a large skillet over medium-high heat until it reaches about 350°F (175°C).
4. Dredge each tomato slice in the flour, shaking off any excess. Dip it into the egg mixture, allowing any excess to drip off, then coat it evenly in the cornmeal or breadcrumbs mixture.
5. Carefully place the breaded tomato slices into the hot oil, working in batches if necessary to avoid overcrowding the skillet. Fry the tomatoes for about 3-4 minutes on each side, or until they are golden brown and crispy.
6. Once the tomatoes are fried, transfer them to a paper towel-lined plate to drain any excess oil.
7. Serve the fried green tomatoes hot as an appetizer, side dish, or as a topping for sandwiches or salads. Enjoy their crispy texture and tangy flavor!

Macaroni and Cheese

Ingredients:

- 8 ounces elbow macaroni or your favorite pasta shape
- 4 tablespoons unsalted butter
- 1/4 cup all-purpose flour
- 2 cups whole milk
- 2 cups shredded sharp cheddar cheese
- 1 cup shredded mozzarella cheese
- 1/2 teaspoon salt
- 1/4 teaspoon black pepper
- 1/4 teaspoon paprika (optional)
- 1/4 cup breadcrumbs (optional, for topping)

Instructions:

1. Preheat your oven to 350°F (175°C). Grease a 9x13-inch baking dish or a similar-sized oven-safe dish.
2. Cook the elbow macaroni according to the package instructions until al dente. Drain and set aside.
3. In a large saucepan, melt the butter over medium heat. Once melted, add the flour and whisk constantly until it forms a smooth paste (roux). Cook the roux for about 1-2 minutes, stirring constantly.
4. Gradually pour in the milk while whisking continuously to prevent lumps from forming. Cook the mixture, stirring frequently, until it thickens and begins to bubble.
5. Reduce the heat to low and stir in the shredded cheddar cheese and shredded mozzarella cheese until melted and smooth. Season the cheese sauce with salt, black pepper, and paprika (if using), adjusting to taste.
6. Add the cooked macaroni to the cheese sauce and stir until well coated.
7. Transfer the macaroni and cheese mixture to the prepared baking dish, spreading it out evenly.
8. If desired, sprinkle breadcrumbs evenly over the top of the macaroni and cheese for a crunchy topping.
9. Bake in the preheated oven for 25-30 minutes, or until the cheese is bubbly and the top is golden brown.

10. Remove the macaroni and cheese from the oven and let it cool for a few minutes before serving. Enjoy this creamy and comforting dish as a main course or side dish!

Corn Chowder

Ingredients:

- 4 slices bacon, chopped
- 1 medium onion, diced
- 2 cloves garlic, minced
- 3 cups fresh or frozen corn kernels
- 2 medium potatoes, peeled and diced
- 3 cups chicken or vegetable broth
- 1 cup milk
- 1/2 cup heavy cream
- 1 bay leaf
- Salt and pepper to taste
- Chopped fresh parsley or chives for garnish (optional)

Instructions:

1. In a large pot or Dutch oven, cook the chopped bacon over medium heat until crispy. Remove the bacon with a slotted spoon and set it aside, leaving the bacon drippings in the pot.
2. Add the diced onion to the pot and cook until softened, about 5 minutes. Add the minced garlic and cook for an additional 1-2 minutes, until fragrant.
3. Stir in the corn kernels and diced potatoes, and cook for another 5 minutes, stirring occasionally.
4. Pour in the chicken or vegetable broth and add the bay leaf. Bring the mixture to a simmer and let it cook for about 15-20 minutes, or until the potatoes are tender.
5. Remove the bay leaf from the pot and discard it. Use an immersion blender to partially blend the soup, leaving some chunks of corn and potatoes for texture. Alternatively, you can transfer a portion of the soup to a blender and blend until smooth, then return it to the pot.
6. Stir in the milk and heavy cream, and season the chowder with salt and pepper to taste. Let it simmer for another 5-10 minutes to heat through and allow the flavors to meld.
7. Serve the corn chowder hot, garnished with the crispy bacon pieces and chopped fresh parsley or chives if desired. Enjoy the creamy and flavorful goodness of this comforting soup!

Meatloaf

Ingredients:

For the meatloaf:

- 1 1/2 pounds ground beef (preferably a mix of lean and fatty meat)
- 1 cup breadcrumbs (fresh or dried)
- 1/2 cup milk
- 1/2 cup finely chopped onion
- 2 cloves garlic, minced
- 2 large eggs, beaten
- 1/4 cup ketchup or tomato sauce
- 1 tablespoon Worcestershire sauce
- 1 teaspoon dried thyme
- 1 teaspoon dried oregano
- 1 teaspoon salt
- 1/2 teaspoon black pepper

For the glaze:

- 1/4 cup ketchup
- 2 tablespoons brown sugar
- 1 tablespoon Dijon mustard

Instructions:

1. Preheat your oven to 350°F (175°C). Lightly grease a 9x5-inch loaf pan or line it with parchment paper.
2. In a large mixing bowl, combine the breadcrumbs and milk. Let them soak for a few minutes until the breadcrumbs are softened.
3. Add the ground beef, chopped onion, minced garlic, beaten eggs, ketchup or tomato sauce, Worcestershire sauce, dried thyme, dried oregano, salt, and black pepper to the bowl with the soaked breadcrumbs. Use your hands or a spoon to mix everything together until well combined.
4. Transfer the meat mixture to the prepared loaf pan, shaping it into a loaf shape.

5. In a small bowl, mix together the ketchup, brown sugar, and Dijon mustard to make the glaze.
6. Spread the glaze evenly over the top of the meatloaf.
7. Bake the meatloaf in the preheated oven for 60-75 minutes, or until it is cooked through and the internal temperature reaches 160°F (71°C) on an instant-read thermometer.
8. Once cooked, remove the meatloaf from the oven and let it rest for a few minutes before slicing and serving.
9. Serve the meatloaf slices hot, accompanied by mashed potatoes, gravy, and your favorite vegetables. Enjoy the comforting flavors of this classic dish!

Deviled Eggs

Ingredients:

- 6 large eggs
- 1/4 cup mayonnaise
- 1 teaspoon Dijon mustard
- 1 teaspoon white vinegar or lemon juice
- 1/2 teaspoon Worcestershire sauce
- Salt and pepper to taste
- Paprika or chopped fresh parsley for garnish (optional)

Instructions:

1. Place the eggs in a single layer in a saucepan and cover them with cold water, ensuring they are fully submerged.
2. Bring the water to a boil over medium-high heat. Once boiling, remove the saucepan from the heat, cover it with a lid, and let the eggs sit in the hot water for 10-12 minutes.
3. After the eggs have cooked, drain the hot water and transfer the eggs to a bowl of ice water to cool for a few minutes.
4. Once the eggs are cool enough to handle, carefully peel them under running water to help remove the shells. Pat the peeled eggs dry with paper towels.
5. Slice each egg in half lengthwise, then gently scoop out the yolks and transfer them to a mixing bowl. Arrange the egg white halves on a serving platter.
6. Mash the egg yolks with a fork until they are smooth and crumbly.
7. Add the mayonnaise, Dijon mustard, white vinegar or lemon juice, Worcestershire sauce, salt, and pepper to the mashed yolks. Stir or whisk until the mixture is smooth and creamy.
8. Taste the filling and adjust the seasonings as needed, adding more salt, pepper, or other seasonings to suit your preference.
9. Spoon or pipe the yolk mixture into the hollowed-out egg white halves, dividing it evenly among them.
10. If desired, sprinkle paprika or chopped fresh parsley over the filled deviled eggs for garnish.
11. Refrigerate the deviled eggs for at least 30 minutes before serving to allow the flavors to meld and the filling to set.

12. Serve the deviled eggs chilled as an appetizer or side dish. Enjoy the creamy and flavorful goodness!

Farmhouse Salad with Homemade Dressing

Ingredients:

For the salad:

- Mixed salad greens (such as lettuce, spinach, arugula, or any other greens of your choice)
- Cherry tomatoes, halved
- Cucumber, sliced
- Red onion, thinly sliced
- Carrots, shredded
- Radishes, thinly sliced
- Optional additional toppings: sliced avocado, boiled eggs, croutons, bacon bits, shredded cheese, etc.

For the dressing:

- 1/4 cup extra virgin olive oil
- 2 tablespoons apple cider vinegar or white wine vinegar
- 1 tablespoon honey or maple syrup
- 1 teaspoon Dijon mustard
- Salt and pepper to taste
- Optional: minced garlic, dried herbs (such as basil, oregano, or thyme)

Instructions:

1. Prepare the salad ingredients by washing and chopping the vegetables as needed. Place them in a large salad bowl or on individual serving plates.
2. In a small bowl or glass jar with a lid, combine the extra virgin olive oil, apple cider vinegar or white wine vinegar, honey or maple syrup, Dijon mustard, salt, pepper, and any optional ingredients like minced garlic or dried herbs. Whisk or shake vigorously until the dressing is well combined.
3. Taste the dressing and adjust the seasoning as needed, adding more salt, pepper, or other ingredients to suit your preference.
4. Drizzle the homemade dressing over the salad greens and vegetables, tossing gently to coat them evenly with the dressing.

5. If desired, add any optional additional toppings such as sliced avocado, boiled eggs, croutons, bacon bits, or shredded cheese.
6. Serve the farmhouse salad immediately as a refreshing and nutritious side dish or light meal. Enjoy the fresh flavors and homemade dressing!

Sourdough Bread

Ingredients:

For the starter:

- 1 cup sourdough starter (active)
- 1 cup all-purpose flour
- 1/2 cup lukewarm water

For the dough:

- 3 1/2 cups all-purpose flour
- 1 1/2 teaspoons salt
- 1 cup lukewarm water
- 1/4 cup sourdough starter (active)

Instructions:

1. Prepare the starter: In a large mixing bowl, combine 1 cup of active sourdough starter, 1 cup of all-purpose flour, and 1/2 cup of lukewarm water. Stir until well combined. Cover the bowl loosely with plastic wrap or a clean kitchen towel and let it sit at room temperature for 8-12 hours or overnight, until bubbly and active.
2. Once the starter is ready, in a separate large mixing bowl, combine 3 1/2 cups of all-purpose flour and 1 1/2 teaspoons of salt.
3. Add 1/4 cup of active sourdough starter to the flour mixture, along with 1 cup of lukewarm water. Stir until a shaggy dough forms.
4. Turn the dough out onto a lightly floured surface and knead it for about 10-15 minutes, until it becomes smooth and elastic. You may need to add a little more flour if the dough is too sticky, or a little more water if it's too dry.
5. Place the kneaded dough in a lightly greased bowl, cover it with plastic wrap or a clean kitchen towel, and let it rise at room temperature for 4-6 hours, or until doubled in size. You can also let it rise in the refrigerator overnight for a slower fermentation process and enhanced flavor.
6. Once the dough has doubled in size, gently deflate it and shape it into a loaf. You can shape it into a round or oval loaf, or place it in a greased loaf pan for a sandwich-style loaf.

7. Place the shaped loaf on a parchment paper-lined baking sheet or in a greased loaf pan. Cover it loosely with plastic wrap or a clean kitchen towel and let it rise at room temperature for another 2-4 hours, or until puffy and almost doubled in size.
8. Preheat your oven to 450°F (230°C). If desired, slash the top of the loaf with a sharp knife or razor blade to create steam vents.
9. Bake the sourdough bread in the preheated oven for 30-40 minutes, or until golden brown and crusty. If you tapped the bottom of the loaf and it sounds hollow, it's done.
10. Remove the bread from the oven and let it cool on a wire rack for at least 30 minutes before slicing and serving. Enjoy the tangy flavor and chewy texture of homemade sourdough bread!

Chicken and Dumplings

Ingredients:

For the chicken:

- 1 whole chicken (about 3-4 pounds), cut into pieces (or use chicken thighs or breasts)
- Salt and pepper to taste
- 2 tablespoons olive oil or butter
- 1 onion, chopped
- 2 carrots, peeled and sliced
- 2 celery stalks, sliced
- 4 cloves garlic, minced
- 6 cups chicken broth
- 1 bay leaf
- 1 teaspoon dried thyme
- 1/2 teaspoon dried rosemary
- 1/2 teaspoon dried parsley

For the dumplings:

- 2 cups all-purpose flour
- 1 tablespoon baking powder
- 1 teaspoon salt
- 1 cup milk
- 4 tablespoons unsalted butter, melted

Instructions:

1. Season the chicken pieces with salt and pepper.
2. In a large pot or Dutch oven, heat the olive oil or butter over medium-high heat. Add the chicken pieces and cook until browned on all sides, about 5-7 minutes per side. Remove the chicken from the pot and set it aside.
3. In the same pot, add the chopped onion, sliced carrots, sliced celery, and minced garlic. Cook, stirring occasionally, until the vegetables are softened, about 5-7 minutes.

4. Return the browned chicken pieces to the pot. Pour in the chicken broth and add the bay leaf, dried thyme, dried rosemary, and dried parsley. Bring the mixture to a simmer, then reduce the heat to low. Cover and let the chicken simmer for about 30-40 minutes, or until it is cooked through and tender.
5. While the chicken is simmering, prepare the dumplings. In a mixing bowl, combine the flour, baking powder, and salt. Stir in the milk and melted butter until a soft dough forms.
6. Once the chicken is cooked, remove it from the pot and shred the meat using two forks. Discard the bones and return the shredded chicken to the pot.
7. Increase the heat to medium-high and bring the broth back to a simmer.
8. Drop spoonfuls of the dumpling dough into the simmering broth, making sure they are evenly spaced. Cover the pot and let the dumplings cook for 15-20 minutes, or until they are cooked through and fluffy.
9. Once the dumplings are cooked, remove the pot from the heat. Taste the broth and adjust the seasoning with salt and pepper if needed.
10. Serve the chicken and dumplings hot, ladled into bowls. Enjoy the comforting and hearty flavors of this classic dish!

Pulled Pork Sandwiches

Ingredients:

For the pork:

- 4-5 pounds pork shoulder (also known as pork butt), trimmed of excess fat
- 2 tablespoons brown sugar
- 1 tablespoon paprika
- 1 tablespoon garlic powder
- 1 tablespoon onion powder
- 1 teaspoon chili powder
- 1 teaspoon cumin
- 1 teaspoon salt
- 1/2 teaspoon black pepper
- 1 cup chicken broth or water
- 1/2 cup apple cider vinegar
- 1/4 cup Worcestershire sauce
- 1/4 cup ketchup
- 2 tablespoons mustard

For the sandwiches:

- Hamburger buns or sandwich rolls
- Coleslaw (optional, for topping)
- Barbecue sauce (optional, for topping)

Instructions:

1. In a small bowl, mix together the brown sugar, paprika, garlic powder, onion powder, chili powder, cumin, salt, and black pepper to make a dry rub.
2. Rub the dry rub mixture all over the pork shoulder, coating it evenly. Let the pork sit at room temperature for about 30 minutes to allow the flavors to penetrate.
3. Preheat your oven to 300°F (150°C).
4. In a roasting pan or Dutch oven, combine the chicken broth or water, apple cider vinegar, Worcestershire sauce, ketchup, and mustard. Place the seasoned pork shoulder in the pan.
5. Cover the pan tightly with aluminum foil or a lid and roast the pork in the preheated oven for 4-5 hours, or until the meat is very tender and falling apart.

6. Once the pork is done, remove it from the oven and let it rest for a few minutes. Use two forks to shred the pork into bite-sized pieces, discarding any large pieces of fat.
7. Serve the pulled pork on hamburger buns or sandwich rolls, topped with coleslaw and barbecue sauce if desired.
8. Enjoy these delicious pulled pork sandwiches with your favorite sides, such as potato salad, corn on the cob, or baked beans.

Collard Greens

Ingredients:

- 2 bunches collard greens (about 2 pounds), washed and trimmed
- 4 slices bacon, chopped
- 1 onion, chopped
- 3 cloves garlic, minced
- 3 cups chicken or vegetable broth
- 1 tablespoon apple cider vinegar or white vinegar
- 1 tablespoon brown sugar or honey
- 1/2 teaspoon red pepper flakes (optional)
- Salt and pepper to taste

Instructions:

1. Stack the collard greens on top of each other and roll them tightly into a cigar shape. Slice the rolled greens crosswise into thin strips.
2. In a large pot or Dutch oven, cook the chopped bacon over medium heat until crispy. Remove the cooked bacon with a slotted spoon and set it aside, leaving the bacon drippings in the pot.
3. Add the chopped onion to the pot and cook until softened, about 5 minutes. Add the minced garlic and cook for an additional 1-2 minutes, until fragrant.
4. Stir in the sliced collard greens and cook until wilted, stirring occasionally, about 5-7 minutes.
5. Pour in the chicken or vegetable broth and add the apple cider vinegar, brown sugar or honey, and red pepper flakes (if using). Stir to combine.
6. Bring the mixture to a simmer, then reduce the heat to low. Cover the pot and let the collard greens simmer gently for about 45 minutes to 1 hour, or until tender.
7. Taste the collard greens and adjust the seasoning with salt and pepper as needed.
8. Once the collard greens are cooked to your desired tenderness, stir in the cooked bacon pieces.
9. Serve the collard greens hot as a side dish or part of a traditional Southern meal. Enjoy their rich flavor and tender texture!

Baked Beans

Ingredients:

- 4 cans (15 ounces each) of navy beans or other white beans, drained and rinsed
- 1/2 cup ketchup
- 1/4 cup molasses
- 1/4 cup brown sugar
- 2 tablespoons mustard (preferably Dijon)
- 1 tablespoon Worcestershire sauce
- 1/2 teaspoon garlic powder
- 1/2 teaspoon onion powder
- 1/4 teaspoon smoked paprika (optional)
- 6 slices bacon, cooked and chopped (optional)
- Salt and black pepper to taste

Instructions:

1. Preheat your oven to 350°F (175°C).
2. In a large mixing bowl, combine the drained and rinsed navy beans with the ketchup, molasses, brown sugar, mustard, Worcestershire sauce, garlic powder, onion powder, and smoked paprika (if using). Stir until all the ingredients are well combined.
3. Taste the bean mixture and adjust the seasoning with salt and black pepper as needed.
4. Transfer the bean mixture to a 9x13-inch baking dish or a similar-sized oven-safe dish.
5. If desired, sprinkle the chopped cooked bacon over the top of the bean mixture for added flavor.
6. Cover the baking dish with aluminum foil and bake in the preheated oven for 45-60 minutes, or until the beans are bubbly and the sauce has thickened to your liking.
7. Remove the foil from the baking dish and continue to bake for an additional 15-20 minutes, or until the top is caramelized and slightly crispy.
8. Remove the baked beans from the oven and let them cool for a few minutes before serving.

9. Serve the baked beans hot as a side dish to grilled meats, barbecue, or any other main dish of your choice. Enjoy the rich, smoky flavor of these classic baked beans!

Pumpkin Pie

Ingredients:

For the pie crust:

- 1 1/4 cups all-purpose flour
- 1/2 teaspoon salt
- 1/2 teaspoon granulated sugar
- 1/2 cup unsalted butter, cold and cut into small pieces
- 3-4 tablespoons ice water

For the filling:

- 1 can (15 ounces) pumpkin puree (not pumpkin pie filling)
- 3/4 cup granulated sugar
- 1 teaspoon ground cinnamon
- 1/2 teaspoon ground ginger
- 1/4 teaspoon ground nutmeg
- 1/4 teaspoon ground cloves
- 1/2 teaspoon salt
- 2 large eggs
- 1 can (12 ounces) evaporated milk

Instructions:

1. Preheat your oven to 375°F (190°C).
2. To make the pie crust, in a large mixing bowl, combine the flour, salt, and granulated sugar. Add the cold butter pieces and use a pastry cutter or your fingers to cut the butter into the flour mixture until it resembles coarse crumbs.
3. Gradually add the ice water, 1 tablespoon at a time, and mix until the dough just begins to come together. Be careful not to overwork the dough. Shape the dough into a disk, wrap it tightly in plastic wrap, and refrigerate it for at least 30 minutes.
4. On a lightly floured surface, roll out the chilled dough into a circle about 12 inches in diameter. Carefully transfer the rolled-out dough to a 9-inch pie dish. Trim any excess dough and crimp the edges as desired. Place the pie dish in the refrigerator while you prepare the filling.

5. In a large mixing bowl, whisk together the pumpkin puree, granulated sugar, ground cinnamon, ground ginger, ground nutmeg, ground cloves, and salt until well combined.
6. Add the eggs to the pumpkin mixture and whisk until smooth.
7. Gradually pour in the evaporated milk, whisking continuously, until the mixture is well combined and smooth.
8. Remove the pie crust from the refrigerator and pour the pumpkin filling into the prepared pie crust.
9. Place the pie in the preheated oven and bake for 15 minutes. Then, reduce the oven temperature to 350°F (175°C) and continue to bake for an additional 45-50 minutes, or until the filling is set and the crust is golden brown.
10. Once done, remove the pie from the oven and let it cool completely on a wire rack before serving.
11. Serve the pumpkin pie at room temperature or chilled, topped with whipped cream or a scoop of vanilla ice cream if desired. Enjoy the rich and creamy flavors of this classic fall dessert!

Chicken Casserole

Ingredients:

- 2 cups cooked chicken, shredded or diced
- 2 cups cooked pasta (such as penne or rotini)
- 1 cup frozen mixed vegetables (such as peas, carrots, and corn)
- 1 can (10.5 ounces) condensed cream of chicken soup
- 1/2 cup sour cream
- 1/2 cup chicken broth
- 1 teaspoon garlic powder
- 1 teaspoon onion powder
- 1/2 teaspoon dried thyme
- Salt and pepper to taste
- 1 cup shredded cheese (such as cheddar or mozzarella)
- 1/2 cup breadcrumbs
- 2 tablespoons melted butter
- Chopped fresh parsley for garnish (optional)

Instructions:

1. Preheat your oven to 375°F (190°C). Lightly grease a 9x13-inch baking dish or similar-sized casserole dish.
2. In a large mixing bowl, combine the cooked chicken, cooked pasta, and frozen mixed vegetables.
3. In a separate bowl, whisk together the condensed cream of chicken soup, sour cream, chicken broth, garlic powder, onion powder, dried thyme, salt, and pepper until well combined.
4. Pour the soup mixture over the chicken, pasta, and vegetables in the mixing bowl. Stir until everything is evenly coated with the sauce.
5. Transfer the mixture to the prepared baking dish and spread it out evenly.
6. Sprinkle the shredded cheese over the top of the casserole.
7. In a small bowl, combine the breadcrumbs and melted butter. Sprinkle the breadcrumb mixture evenly over the cheese layer.
8. Cover the baking dish with aluminum foil and bake in the preheated oven for 20 minutes.

9. After 20 minutes, remove the foil from the baking dish and continue to bake for an additional 10-15 minutes, or until the casserole is bubbly and the cheese is melted and golden brown.
10. Once done, remove the casserole from the oven and let it cool for a few minutes before serving.
11. Garnish with chopped fresh parsley if desired, and serve the chicken casserole hot as a comforting and satisfying meal. Enjoy!

Tomato Soup

Ingredients:

- 2 tablespoons olive oil
- 1 onion, chopped
- 2 cloves garlic, minced
- 2 cans (28 ounces each) whole peeled tomatoes
- 2 cups vegetable or chicken broth
- 1 teaspoon sugar
- 1/2 teaspoon dried basil
- 1/2 teaspoon dried oregano
- Salt and pepper to taste
- 1/2 cup heavy cream or half-and-half (optional)
- Fresh basil leaves for garnish (optional)
- Croutons or grated cheese for serving (optional)

Instructions:

1. In a large pot or Dutch oven, heat the olive oil over medium heat. Add the chopped onion and cook until softened, about 5 minutes.
2. Add the minced garlic to the pot and cook for an additional 1-2 minutes, until fragrant.
3. Pour the whole peeled tomatoes into the pot, along with their juices. Use a wooden spoon to break up the tomatoes into smaller pieces.
4. Add the vegetable or chicken broth to the pot, along with the sugar, dried basil, dried oregano, salt, and pepper. Stir to combine.
5. Bring the soup to a simmer, then reduce the heat to low. Let the soup simmer gently, uncovered, for about 20-30 minutes, stirring occasionally, to allow the flavors to meld.
6. Once the soup has simmered and thickened slightly, remove it from the heat. If desired, use an immersion blender to puree the soup until smooth. Alternatively, you can transfer the soup to a blender and blend in batches until smooth, then return it to the pot.
7. Stir in the heavy cream or half-and-half, if using, until well combined. Taste the soup and adjust the seasoning with salt and pepper as needed.

8. Ladle the tomato soup into bowls and garnish with fresh basil leaves, if desired. Serve hot, topped with croutons or grated cheese if desired. Enjoy the comforting and delicious flavors of homemade tomato soup!

Cornbread Stuffing

Ingredients:

For the cornbread:

- 1 cup cornmeal
- 1 cup all-purpose flour
- 1 tablespoon baking powder
- 1 teaspoon salt
- 1 cup buttermilk
- 1/4 cup unsalted butter, melted
- 1/4 cup honey or maple syrup
- 2 large eggs

For the stuffing:

- 4 cups cubed cornbread (about 1/2-inch cubes)
- 4 tablespoons unsalted butter
- 1 onion, chopped
- 2 celery stalks, chopped
- 2 cloves garlic, minced
- 1 teaspoon dried sage
- 1 teaspoon dried thyme
- 1/2 teaspoon dried rosemary
- Salt and pepper to taste
- 1/2 cup chicken or vegetable broth, plus more as needed

Instructions:

1. Preheat your oven to 375°F (190°C). Grease a 9x13-inch baking dish or similar-sized casserole dish.
2. To make the cornbread, in a large mixing bowl, combine the cornmeal, all-purpose flour, baking powder, and salt.
3. In a separate bowl, whisk together the buttermilk, melted butter, honey or maple syrup, and eggs until well combined.
4. Pour the wet ingredients into the dry ingredients and stir until just combined. Be careful not to overmix.

5. Pour the cornbread batter into a greased 9x9-inch baking dish and spread it out evenly. Bake in the preheated oven for 20-25 minutes, or until a toothpick inserted into the center comes out clean. Remove the cornbread from the oven and let it cool completely. Once cooled, cut it into 1/2-inch cubes.
6. In a large skillet, melt the butter over medium heat. Add the chopped onion and celery, and cook until softened, about 5-7 minutes.
7. Add the minced garlic, dried sage, dried thyme, and dried rosemary to the skillet, and cook for an additional 1-2 minutes, until fragrant.
8. Stir in the cubed cornbread and mix until well combined with the onion and celery mixture. Season with salt and pepper to taste.
9. Gradually pour the chicken or vegetable broth over the cornbread mixture, stirring gently to moisten the ingredients evenly. Add more broth as needed to reach your desired consistency.
10. Transfer the cornbread stuffing mixture to the prepared baking dish, spreading it out evenly.
11. Cover the baking dish with aluminum foil and bake in the preheated oven for 20-25 minutes.
12. Remove the foil from the baking dish and continue to bake for an additional 10-15 minutes, or until the top is golden brown and crispy.
13. Once done, remove the cornbread stuffing from the oven and let it cool for a few minutes before serving.
14. Serve the cornbread stuffing hot as a delicious side dish for Thanksgiving or any other holiday meal. Enjoy the savory flavors and hearty texture!

Blackberry Cobbler

Ingredients:

For the filling:

- 6 cups fresh blackberries
- 1/2 cup granulated sugar (adjust according to the sweetness of the berries)
- 2 tablespoons cornstarch
- 1 tablespoon lemon juice
- Zest of 1 lemon

For the topping:

- 1 1/2 cups all-purpose flour
- 1/2 cup granulated sugar
- 1 1/2 teaspoons baking powder
- 1/2 teaspoon salt
- 1/2 cup unsalted butter, cold and cut into small pieces
- 1/2 cup milk
- 1 teaspoon vanilla extract

Instructions:

1. Preheat your oven to 375°F (190°C). Lightly grease a 9x13-inch baking dish or similar-sized casserole dish.
2. In a large mixing bowl, combine the fresh blackberries, granulated sugar, cornstarch, lemon juice, and lemon zest. Gently toss until the blackberries are evenly coated. Transfer the blackberry mixture to the prepared baking dish and spread it out evenly.
3. In a separate mixing bowl, combine the all-purpose flour, granulated sugar, baking powder, and salt. Stir until well combined.
4. Add the cold, diced butter to the flour mixture. Use a pastry cutter or your fingers to cut the butter into the flour mixture until it resembles coarse crumbs.
5. In a small bowl, whisk together the milk and vanilla extract. Gradually pour the milk mixture into the flour mixture, stirring until just combined. Be careful not to overmix.
6. Drop spoonfuls of the biscuit topping over the blackberry filling in the baking dish, covering it evenly.

7. Bake the cobbler in the preheated oven for 35-40 minutes, or until the topping is golden brown and the blackberry filling is bubbly.
8. Once done, remove the cobbler from the oven and let it cool for a few minutes before serving.
9. Serve the blackberry cobbler warm, topped with a scoop of vanilla ice cream or a dollop of whipped cream if desired. Enjoy the sweet and tangy flavors of this classic dessert!

Mashed Potatoes

Ingredients:

- 2 pounds potatoes (such as Russet or Yukon Gold), peeled and cut into chunks
- 4 tablespoons unsalted butter
- 1/2 cup milk or heavy cream
- Salt and pepper to taste
- Chopped fresh parsley or chives for garnish (optional)

Instructions:

1. Place the potato chunks in a large pot and cover them with cold water. Add a generous pinch of salt to the water.
2. Bring the water to a boil over medium-high heat. Reduce the heat to medium-low and simmer the potatoes for 15-20 minutes, or until they are fork-tender.
3. Drain the cooked potatoes and return them to the pot.
4. Add the butter to the pot with the hot potatoes. Let the butter melt slightly.
5. Mash the potatoes and butter together using a potato masher or a fork until they reach your desired consistency. Some prefer smooth mashed potatoes, while others prefer them slightly chunky.
6. Gradually add the milk or heavy cream to the mashed potatoes, stirring continuously, until the desired creaminess is achieved. You may need more or less milk/cream depending on your preference.
7. Season the mashed potatoes with salt and pepper to taste. Stir well to combine.
8. Transfer the mashed potatoes to a serving dish and garnish with chopped fresh parsley or chives if desired.
9. Serve the mashed potatoes hot as a delicious side dish to accompany your favorite main courses. Enjoy the creamy and comforting flavors of homemade mashed potatoes!

Beef Pot Roast

Ingredients:

- 1 (3-4 pound) beef chuck roast
- Salt and pepper to taste
- 2 tablespoons vegetable oil or olive oil
- 1 onion, chopped
- 2 carrots, peeled and chopped into chunks
- 2 celery stalks, chopped into chunks
- 4 cloves garlic, minced
- 1 cup beef broth
- 1/2 cup red wine (optional)
- 2 tablespoons tomato paste
- 2 bay leaves
- 1 teaspoon dried thyme
- 1 teaspoon dried rosemary
- 1 teaspoon dried oregano
- 1 pound potatoes, peeled and chopped into chunks

Instructions:

1. Preheat your oven to 325°F (160°C).
2. Season the beef chuck roast generously with salt and pepper on all sides.
3. In a large Dutch oven or oven-safe pot, heat the vegetable oil or olive oil over medium-high heat. Add the seasoned beef chuck roast and sear it on all sides until browned, about 3-4 minutes per side. Remove the seared roast from the pot and set it aside.
4. In the same pot, add the chopped onion, carrots, and celery. Cook, stirring occasionally, until the vegetables are softened, about 5 minutes.
5. Add the minced garlic to the pot and cook for an additional 1-2 minutes, until fragrant.
6. Return the seared beef chuck roast to the pot, nestling it among the vegetables.
7. In a mixing bowl, combine the beef broth, red wine (if using), tomato paste, bay leaves, dried thyme, dried rosemary, and dried oregano. Stir until well combined.
8. Pour the broth mixture over the beef roast and vegetables in the pot, covering them as much as possible.

9. Cover the pot with a lid and transfer it to the preheated oven. Let the beef roast cook in the oven for about 2 1/2 to 3 hours, or until the meat is tender and easily shreds with a fork.
10. About 30 minutes before the roast is done cooking, add the chopped potatoes to the pot, nestling them around the beef roast and vegetables.
11. Once the beef roast and potatoes are cooked to your liking, remove the pot from the oven.
12. Transfer the beef roast to a cutting board and let it rest for a few minutes before slicing it against the grain.
13. Serve the sliced beef pot roast and vegetables hot, accompanied by the flavorful cooking juices from the pot. Enjoy the tender and savory flavors of this classic comfort food dish!

Fried Catfish

Ingredients:

- 4 catfish fillets
- 1 cup cornmeal or all-purpose flour
- 1 teaspoon salt
- 1/2 teaspoon black pepper
- 1/2 teaspoon paprika
- 1/4 teaspoon cayenne pepper (optional, for added heat)
- Vegetable oil for frying
- Lemon wedges for serving
- Tartar sauce or remoulade sauce for serving (optional)

Instructions:

1. Rinse the catfish fillets under cold water and pat them dry with paper towels.
2. In a shallow dish or bowl, combine the cornmeal or flour, salt, black pepper, paprika, and cayenne pepper (if using). Stir until well combined.
3. Dredge each catfish fillet in the seasoned cornmeal or flour mixture, coating both sides evenly. Shake off any excess coating.
4. Heat vegetable oil in a large skillet or frying pan over medium-high heat until it reaches 350°F (175°C).
5. Carefully place the coated catfish fillets into the hot oil, making sure not to overcrowd the pan. You may need to fry the fillets in batches, depending on the size of your skillet.
6. Fry the catfish fillets for 3-4 minutes on each side, or until they are golden brown and crispy. Use a spatula to carefully flip the fillets halfway through cooking.
7. Once the catfish fillets are cooked through and crispy on the outside, remove them from the oil and transfer them to a plate lined with paper towels to drain any excess oil.
8. Serve the fried catfish hot, garnished with lemon wedges and accompanied by tartar sauce or remoulade sauce if desired.
9. Enjoy the crispy and flavorful fried catfish as a delicious main dish, served with your favorite sides such as coleslaw, hush puppies, or french fries.

Green Bean Casserole

Ingredients:

- 1 1/2 pounds green beans, trimmed and halved
- 1 can (10.5 ounces) condensed cream of mushroom soup
- 1/2 cup milk
- 1 teaspoon soy sauce
- 1/4 teaspoon black pepper
- 1 cup crispy fried onions (French's Fried Onions)
- Salt to taste (optional)
- Optional additional toppings: shredded cheese, cooked and crumbled bacon, sliced mushrooms

Instructions:

1. Preheat your oven to 350°F (175°C). Grease a 9x13-inch baking dish or similar-sized casserole dish.
2. Bring a large pot of salted water to a boil. Add the green beans and cook for 4-5 minutes, or until just tender. Drain the green beans and transfer them to a large bowl of ice water to stop the cooking process. Drain again and set aside.
3. In a separate mixing bowl, combine the condensed cream of mushroom soup, milk, soy sauce, and black pepper. Stir until well combined.
4. Add the cooked green beans to the soup mixture and toss until the green beans are evenly coated.
5. Transfer the green bean mixture to the prepared baking dish and spread it out evenly.
6. Bake the green bean casserole in the preheated oven for 25-30 minutes, or until the mixture is hot and bubbly.
7. Remove the casserole from the oven and sprinkle the crispy fried onions evenly over the top.
8. Return the casserole to the oven and bake for an additional 5 minutes, or until the onions are golden brown and crispy.
9. Once done, remove the casserole from the oven and let it cool for a few minutes before serving.
10. Serve the green bean casserole hot as a delicious side dish for Thanksgiving, Christmas, or any other holiday meal. Enjoy the classic flavors and comforting texture of this timeless dish!

Potato Salad

Ingredients:

- 2 pounds potatoes (such as Yukon Gold or red potatoes), peeled and cut into chunks
- 4 large eggs
- 1 cup mayonnaise
- 2 tablespoons Dijon mustard
- 2 tablespoons apple cider vinegar
- 1/2 cup chopped celery
- 1/4 cup chopped red onion
- 2 tablespoons chopped fresh parsley
- Salt and black pepper to taste
- Paprika for garnish (optional)

Instructions:

1. Place the potato chunks in a large pot and cover them with cold water. Add a generous pinch of salt to the water. Bring the water to a boil over medium-high heat, then reduce the heat to medium-low and simmer the potatoes for 10-15 minutes, or until they are fork-tender.
2. While the potatoes are cooking, place the eggs in a separate pot and cover them with cold water. Bring the water to a boil, then remove the pot from the heat, cover it with a lid, and let the eggs sit in the hot water for 10-12 minutes. Drain the hot water and transfer the eggs to a bowl of ice water to cool.
3. Once the potatoes are cooked, drain them and let them cool slightly.
4. Peel the cooled hard-boiled eggs and chop them into small pieces.
5. In a large mixing bowl, whisk together the mayonnaise, Dijon mustard, and apple cider vinegar until smooth.
6. Add the cooked potato chunks, chopped hard-boiled eggs, chopped celery, chopped red onion, and chopped parsley to the bowl with the dressing. Gently toss until all the ingredients are evenly coated with the dressing.
7. Season the potato salad with salt and black pepper to taste.
8. Transfer the potato salad to a serving dish and sprinkle with paprika for garnish, if desired.
9. Cover the potato salad and refrigerate it for at least 1 hour before serving to allow the flavors to meld.

10. Serve the potato salad chilled as a delicious side dish for picnics, barbecues, or any occasion. Enjoy the creamy and flavorful combination of potatoes, eggs, and fresh herbs!

Banana Bread

Ingredients:

- 2 to 3 ripe bananas, mashed
- 1/3 cup unsalted butter, melted
- 3/4 cup granulated sugar
- 1 large egg, beaten
- 1 teaspoon vanilla extract
- 1 teaspoon baking soda
- Pinch of salt
- 1 1/2 cups all-purpose flour

Optional add-ins:

- 1/2 cup chopped nuts (such as walnuts or pecans)
- 1/2 cup chocolate chips
- 1/2 cup dried fruit (such as raisins or chopped dates)

Instructions:

1. Preheat your oven to 350°F (175°C). Grease a 9x5-inch loaf pan or line it with parchment paper.
2. In a large mixing bowl, mash the ripe bananas with a fork until smooth.
3. Stir the melted butter into the mashed bananas.
4. Add the granulated sugar, beaten egg, and vanilla extract to the banana mixture. Stir until well combined.
5. Sprinkle the baking soda and salt over the banana mixture, then gently mix them in.
6. Add the all-purpose flour to the banana mixture and stir until just combined. Be careful not to overmix.
7. If using any optional add-ins such as chopped nuts, chocolate chips, or dried fruit, fold them into the batter until evenly distributed.
8. Pour the batter into the prepared loaf pan and spread it out evenly.
9. Bake the banana bread in the preheated oven for 50-60 minutes, or until a toothpick inserted into the center comes out clean.
10. Once done, remove the banana bread from the oven and let it cool in the loaf pan for 10 minutes.

11. Carefully transfer the banana bread to a wire rack to cool completely before slicing and serving.
12. Serve the banana bread slices warm or at room temperature. Enjoy the moist and flavorful goodness of homemade banana bread!

Ham and Bean Soup

Ingredients:

- 1 tablespoon olive oil
- 1 onion, chopped
- 2 carrots, peeled and chopped
- 2 celery stalks, chopped
- 2 cloves garlic, minced
- 1 ham bone or 1 pound ham hock
- 1 pound dried navy beans or Great Northern beans, rinsed and soaked overnight
- 8 cups chicken or vegetable broth
- 2 bay leaves
- 1 teaspoon dried thyme
- Salt and pepper to taste
- Chopped fresh parsley for garnish (optional)

Instructions:

1. Heat the olive oil in a large pot or Dutch oven over medium heat. Add the chopped onion, carrots, and celery. Cook, stirring occasionally, until the vegetables are softened, about 5-7 minutes.
2. Add the minced garlic to the pot and cook for an additional 1-2 minutes, until fragrant.
3. Place the ham bone or ham hock in the pot with the vegetables.
4. Drain and rinse the soaked beans, then add them to the pot.
5. Pour the chicken or vegetable broth into the pot, ensuring that the ingredients are submerged. Add the bay leaves and dried thyme.
6. Bring the soup to a boil, then reduce the heat to low. Cover the pot and let the soup simmer gently for 1 1/2 to 2 hours, or until the beans are tender and the meat is falling off the bone.
7. Once the beans are cooked through, remove the ham bone or ham hock from the pot. Remove any meat from the bone and chop it into bite-sized pieces. Discard any fat or gristle.
8. Return the chopped ham meat to the pot. Season the soup with salt and pepper to taste, adjusting as needed.
9. If desired, use an immersion blender to partially blend the soup for a thicker consistency, or leave it chunky.

10. Ladle the ham and bean soup into bowls and garnish with chopped fresh parsley if desired.
11. Serve the soup hot, accompanied by crusty bread or cornbread for a hearty and satisfying meal. Enjoy the rich flavors and comforting warmth of this homemade ham and bean soup!

Fried Chicken Livers

Ingredients:

- 1 pound chicken livers, trimmed and cleaned
- 1 cup buttermilk
- 1 cup all-purpose flour
- 1 teaspoon salt
- 1/2 teaspoon black pepper
- 1/2 teaspoon paprika
- Vegetable oil, for frying

Instructions:

1. Place the cleaned chicken livers in a bowl and pour the buttermilk over them. Make sure the livers are well coated. Cover the bowl and let the livers marinate in the buttermilk for at least 30 minutes to 1 hour in the refrigerator. This helps to tenderize the livers and adds flavor.
2. In a shallow dish or bowl, combine the all-purpose flour, salt, black pepper, and paprika. Stir until well combined.
3. Heat vegetable oil in a large skillet or frying pan over medium-high heat until it reaches 350°F (175°C).
4. Remove the chicken livers from the buttermilk marinade, allowing any excess buttermilk to drip off.
5. Dredge the chicken livers in the seasoned flour mixture, coating them evenly on all sides.
6. Carefully place the coated chicken livers in the hot oil, making sure not to overcrowd the pan. Fry the livers in batches if necessary.
7. Fry the chicken livers for about 3-4 minutes per side, or until they are golden brown and cooked through. Use tongs to flip them halfway through cooking.
8. Once the chicken livers are cooked, remove them from the oil and transfer them to a plate lined with paper towels to drain any excess oil.
9. Serve the fried chicken livers hot as a delicious appetizer or main dish. Enjoy them on their own or with your favorite dipping sauce. They pair well with mashed potatoes, coleslaw, or a side salad.

Corn Pudding

Ingredients:

- 4 cups fresh or frozen corn kernels (about 6-8 ears of corn)
- 4 large eggs
- 1/4 cup unsalted butter, melted
- 1/4 cup granulated sugar
- 1/4 cup all-purpose flour
- 1 teaspoon baking powder
- 1 teaspoon salt
- 1 cup milk
- 1/2 cup heavy cream
- Optional: 1/4 cup chopped fresh herbs (such as parsley or chives)

Instructions:

1. Preheat your oven to 350°F (175°C). Grease a 9x13-inch baking dish or similar-sized casserole dish.
2. If using fresh corn, cut the kernels off the cobs. If using frozen corn, thaw it according to package instructions.
3. In a large mixing bowl, whisk together the eggs, melted butter, and granulated sugar until well combined.
4. In a separate bowl, combine the all-purpose flour, baking powder, and salt. Gradually add the flour mixture to the egg mixture, stirring until smooth.
5. Stir in the milk and heavy cream until the batter is smooth and well combined.
6. Fold the corn kernels into the batter until evenly distributed. If using chopped fresh herbs, fold them into the batter as well.
7. Pour the corn pudding batter into the prepared baking dish, spreading it out evenly.
8. Bake the corn pudding in the preheated oven for 45-55 minutes, or until the top is golden brown and the pudding is set in the center. It should have a slight jiggle, similar to a custard.
9. Once done, remove the corn pudding from the oven and let it cool for a few minutes before serving.
10. Serve the corn pudding warm as a delicious side dish for any meal. It pairs well with roasted meats, grilled vegetables, or as part of a holiday spread. Enjoy the creamy and comforting flavors of this classic dish!

Lemonade

Ingredients:

- 1 cup freshly squeezed lemon juice (about 4-6 lemons)
- 3/4 cup granulated sugar (adjust to taste)
- 4 cups cold water
- Ice cubes
- Lemon slices and fresh mint leaves for garnish (optional)

Instructions:

1. Start by making a simple syrup. In a small saucepan, combine 1 cup of water with the granulated sugar. Heat over medium heat, stirring occasionally, until the sugar has completely dissolved. This will create a sweet syrup for your lemonade.
2. While the sugar is dissolving, squeeze enough lemons to yield 1 cup of freshly squeezed lemon juice. This usually requires about 4 to 6 lemons, depending on their size and juiciness.
3. In a large pitcher, combine the freshly squeezed lemon juice with the simple syrup. Stir well to combine.
4. Add 3 cups of cold water to the pitcher and stir again. Taste the lemonade and adjust the sweetness or tartness by adding more water or sugar if needed.
5. Refrigerate the lemonade for at least 30 minutes to chill it thoroughly.
6. Once chilled, fill glasses with ice cubes and pour the lemonade over the ice.
7. Garnish each glass with a slice of lemon and a sprig of fresh mint, if desired.
8. Serve the homemade lemonade immediately and enjoy its refreshing citrus flavor!

Feel free to customize your lemonade by adding other fruits like strawberries or raspberries for a twist. You can also experiment with herbs like basil or thyme for unique flavor combinations.

Apple Crisp

Ingredients:

For the filling:

- 6 cups peeled, cored, and sliced apples (about 6 medium-sized apples)
- 1/4 cup granulated sugar
- 2 tablespoons all-purpose flour
- 1 teaspoon ground cinnamon
- 1/4 teaspoon ground nutmeg
- 1 tablespoon lemon juice

For the topping:

- 3/4 cup old-fashioned rolled oats
- 1/2 cup all-purpose flour
- 1/2 cup packed brown sugar
- 1/4 teaspoon salt
- 1/2 cup unsalted butter, cold and cut into small cubes

Instructions:

1. Preheat your oven to 375°F (190°C). Grease a 9x9-inch baking dish or similar-sized casserole dish.
2. In a large mixing bowl, combine the sliced apples, granulated sugar, all-purpose flour, ground cinnamon, ground nutmeg, and lemon juice. Toss until the apples are evenly coated with the sugar and spice mixture.
3. Transfer the apple mixture to the prepared baking dish and spread it out evenly.
4. In a separate mixing bowl, combine the rolled oats, all-purpose flour, brown sugar, and salt for the topping. Stir until well combined.
5. Add the cold, cubed butter to the oat mixture. Use a pastry cutter or your fingers to cut the butter into the dry ingredients until the mixture resembles coarse crumbs.
6. Sprinkle the oat topping evenly over the apples in the baking dish, covering them completely.
7. Bake the apple crisp in the preheated oven for 35-40 minutes, or until the topping is golden brown and the apples are tender and bubbly.

8. Once done, remove the apple crisp from the oven and let it cool for a few minutes before serving.
9. Serve the apple crisp warm, topped with a scoop of vanilla ice cream or a dollop of whipped cream if desired. Enjoy the sweet and comforting flavors of homemade apple crisp!

Shepherd's Pie

Ingredients:

For the mashed potato topping:

- 2 pounds potatoes (such as Russet or Yukon Gold), peeled and cut into chunks
- 4 tablespoons unsalted butter
- 1/2 cup milk or heavy cream
- Salt and pepper to taste

For the filling:

- 1 tablespoon olive oil
- 1 onion, chopped
- 2 carrots, peeled and diced
- 2 cloves garlic, minced
- 1 pound ground lamb or beef
- 2 tablespoons all-purpose flour
- 1 cup beef or vegetable broth
- 1 tablespoon Worcestershire sauce
- 1 teaspoon dried thyme
- 1 teaspoon dried rosemary
- Salt and pepper to taste
- 1 cup frozen peas
- Chopped fresh parsley for garnish (optional)

Instructions:

1. Preheat your oven to 375°F (190°C). Grease a 9x13-inch baking dish or similar-sized casserole dish.
2. Place the peeled and chopped potatoes in a large pot and cover them with cold water. Add a generous pinch of salt to the water. Bring the water to a boil over medium-high heat, then reduce the heat to medium-low and simmer the potatoes for 15-20 minutes, or until they are fork-tender.
3. While the potatoes are cooking, heat the olive oil in a large skillet over medium heat. Add the chopped onion and diced carrots, and cook until softened, about 5-7 minutes. Add the minced garlic and cook for an additional 1-2 minutes, until fragrant.

4. Add the ground lamb or beef to the skillet with the cooked vegetables. Cook, breaking up the meat with a spoon, until browned and cooked through.
5. Sprinkle the flour over the meat and vegetable mixture, stirring to coat evenly. Cook for 1-2 minutes to cook off the raw flour taste.
6. Pour in the beef or vegetable broth and Worcestershire sauce, stirring to combine. Add the dried thyme, dried rosemary, salt, and pepper. Bring the mixture to a simmer and cook for a few minutes until thickened slightly.
7. Stir in the frozen peas, then remove the skillet from the heat.
8. Once the potatoes are cooked, drain them and return them to the pot. Add the butter and milk or heavy cream to the pot with the hot potatoes. Mash the potatoes until smooth and creamy. Season with salt and pepper to taste.
9. Transfer the meat and vegetable mixture to the prepared baking dish and spread it out evenly.
10. Spoon the mashed potatoes over the top of the meat mixture, spreading them out evenly to cover the filling.
11. Use a fork to create a decorative pattern on the surface of the mashed potatoes, if desired.
12. Place the baking dish in the preheated oven and bake for 25-30 minutes, or until the filling is bubbly and the mashed potatoes are golden brown on top.
13. Once done, remove the Shepherd's Pie from the oven and let it cool for a few minutes before serving.
14. Garnish with chopped fresh parsley, if desired, before serving. Enjoy the comforting and hearty flavors of homemade Shepherd's Pie!

Cabbage Rolls

Ingredients:

For the cabbage rolls:

- 1 large head of cabbage
- 1 pound ground beef or a mixture of ground beef and pork
- 1 cup cooked rice
- 1 small onion, finely chopped
- 2 cloves garlic, minced
- 1 egg, beaten
- 1 teaspoon salt
- 1/2 teaspoon black pepper
- 1/2 teaspoon paprika
- 1/4 teaspoon ground nutmeg
- 1/4 teaspoon dried thyme
- 1/4 cup chopped fresh parsley
- 1 (14.5-ounce) can diced tomatoes, undrained

For the tomato sauce:

- 1 (14.5-ounce) can crushed tomatoes
- 1 tablespoon brown sugar
- 1 tablespoon apple cider vinegar
- Salt and pepper to taste

Instructions:

1. Bring a large pot of water to a boil. Carefully remove the core from the cabbage and place the whole head of cabbage in the boiling water. Cook for about 5-7 minutes, or until the outer leaves are softened and can be easily removed. Use tongs to carefully remove the leaves as they soften, transferring them to a plate to cool. Repeat until you have about 12 large leaves.
2. In a mixing bowl, combine the ground beef, cooked rice, chopped onion, minced garlic, beaten egg, salt, black pepper, paprika, ground nutmeg, dried thyme, and chopped fresh parsley. Mix until well combined.

3. Place about 1/4 cup of the meat and rice mixture in the center of each cabbage leaf. Roll the leaf tightly around the filling, tucking in the sides as you roll. Place the cabbage rolls seam side down in a large baking dish or casserole dish.
4. Pour the diced tomatoes over the top of the cabbage rolls in the baking dish.
5. In a separate bowl, mix together the crushed tomatoes, brown sugar, apple cider vinegar, salt, and pepper to make the tomato sauce. Pour the sauce over the cabbage rolls in the baking dish, covering them evenly.
6. Cover the baking dish with aluminum foil and bake in a preheated 350°F (175°C) oven for 1 to 1 1/2 hours, or until the cabbage rolls are cooked through and tender.
7. Once done, remove the foil from the baking dish and let the cabbage rolls cool for a few minutes before serving.
8. Serve the cabbage rolls hot, spooning some of the tomato sauce over the top. Enjoy the savory and comforting flavors of homemade cabbage rolls!

Pickled Beets

Ingredients:

- 3-4 medium-sized beets, washed and trimmed
- 1 cup apple cider vinegar
- 1/2 cup water
- 1/4 cup granulated sugar
- 1 teaspoon salt
- 1 teaspoon whole black peppercorns
- 1 teaspoon whole cloves
- 1 bay leaf
- Optional: additional herbs and spices such as cinnamon sticks, star anise, or fresh thyme sprigs

Instructions:

1. Preheat your oven to 400°F (200°C). Wrap each beet individually in aluminum foil and place them on a baking sheet.
2. Roast the beets in the preheated oven for 45-60 minutes, or until they are tender when pierced with a fork. The cooking time will depend on the size of the beets.
3. Once the beets are cooked, remove them from the oven and let them cool until they are comfortable to handle.
4. While the beets are cooling, prepare the pickling liquid. In a small saucepan, combine the apple cider vinegar, water, granulated sugar, salt, whole black peppercorns, whole cloves, and bay leaf. Bring the mixture to a simmer over medium heat, stirring occasionally, until the sugar and salt are completely dissolved. Remove the saucepan from the heat and let the pickling liquid cool slightly.
5. Once the beets are cool enough to handle, use your fingers or a paper towel to rub off the skins. They should peel off easily. Slice the peeled beets into rounds or wedges, depending on your preference.
6. Pack the sliced beets into clean, sterilized jars, leaving some space at the top.
7. Pour the warm pickling liquid over the beets in the jars, making sure they are completely submerged. If using additional herbs and spices, add them to the jars as well.
8. Seal the jars with lids and let them cool to room temperature.
9. Once cooled, refrigerate the pickled beets for at least 24 hours before serving to allow the flavors to develop.

10. Serve the pickled beets as a tangy and flavorful side dish, salad topping, or sandwich ingredient. Enjoy the delicious taste of homemade pickled beets!

Grits

Ingredients:

- 1 cup stone-ground grits
- 4 cups water
- 1 teaspoon salt
- 2 tablespoons butter
- Optional toppings: shredded cheese, cooked bacon or sausage, chopped green onions, hot sauce

Instructions:

1. In a medium-sized saucepan, bring the water to a boil over high heat.
2. Once the water is boiling, slowly whisk in the grits, stirring continuously to prevent clumping.
3. Reduce the heat to low and add the salt. Stir the grits frequently to prevent sticking and cook them at a gentle simmer for about 20-25 minutes, or until they are thickened and creamy. Be sure to scrape the bottom of the pan to prevent the grits from sticking.
4. Once the grits have reached your desired consistency, remove the saucepan from the heat.
5. Stir in the butter until melted and well incorporated.
6. Serve the creamy grits hot, topped with your choice of optional toppings such as shredded cheese, cooked bacon or sausage, chopped green onions, or a drizzle of hot sauce.
7. Enjoy the comforting and delicious flavors of homemade Southern-style grits as a side dish for breakfast, brunch, or any meal of the day!

Biscuits and Gravy

Ingredients:

For the biscuits:

- 2 cups all-purpose flour
- 1 tablespoon baking powder
- 1 teaspoon salt
- 1/2 cup unsalted butter, cold and cut into small cubes
- 3/4 cup milk

For the sausage gravy:

- 1 pound breakfast sausage (such as pork or turkey sausage)
- 1/4 cup all-purpose flour
- 3 cups milk
- Salt and pepper to taste

Instructions:

1. Preheat your oven to 425°F (220°C). Line a baking sheet with parchment paper or grease it lightly.
2. In a large mixing bowl, whisk together the flour, baking powder, and salt.
3. Add the cold, cubed butter to the flour mixture. Use a pastry cutter or your fingers to cut the butter into the flour until the mixture resembles coarse crumbs.
4. Gradually add the milk to the flour mixture, stirring until a soft dough forms. Be careful not to overmix.
5. Turn the dough out onto a lightly floured surface. Pat or roll the dough to a thickness of about 1/2 inch.
6. Use a biscuit cutter or a round glass to cut out biscuits from the dough. Place the biscuits on the prepared baking sheet, leaving a little space between each biscuit.
7. Bake the biscuits in the preheated oven for 12-15 minutes, or until they are golden brown and cooked through.
8. While the biscuits are baking, prepare the sausage gravy. In a large skillet or frying pan, cook the breakfast sausage over medium heat, breaking it up with a spoon, until it is browned and cooked through.

9. Sprinkle the cooked sausage with flour and stir to coat evenly. Cook for 1-2 minutes to cook off the raw flour taste.
10. Gradually pour the milk into the skillet with the sausage, stirring constantly to prevent lumps from forming.
11. Continue cooking the gravy, stirring frequently, until it thickens to your desired consistency. This usually takes about 5-7 minutes.
12. Season the sausage gravy with salt and pepper to taste.
13. Once the biscuits are done baking, remove them from the oven and let them cool for a few minutes.
14. Split the biscuits in half and place them on serving plates. Spoon the warm sausage gravy over the biscuits.
15. Serve the biscuits and gravy hot as a comforting and hearty breakfast or brunch dish. Enjoy the delicious flavors of homemade biscuits and gravy!

Chicken Fried Rice

Ingredients:

- 2 cups cooked white rice (preferably chilled or leftover)
- 2 tablespoons vegetable oil
- 2 boneless, skinless chicken breasts, diced
- 2 cloves garlic, minced
- 1 small onion, diced
- 1 cup mixed vegetables (such as peas, carrots, and corn)
- 2 eggs, lightly beaten
- 3 tablespoons soy sauce
- 1 tablespoon oyster sauce (optional)
- Salt and pepper to taste
- Chopped green onions for garnish (optional)
- Sesame seeds for garnish (optional)

Instructions:

1. Heat 1 tablespoon of vegetable oil in a large skillet or wok over medium-high heat. Add the diced chicken breasts and season with salt and pepper. Cook the chicken until it is browned and cooked through, about 5-6 minutes. Remove the chicken from the skillet and set it aside.
2. In the same skillet, add another tablespoon of vegetable oil. Add the minced garlic and diced onion, and cook until they are softened and fragrant, about 2-3 minutes.
3. Add the mixed vegetables to the skillet and cook until they are heated through, about 2-3 minutes.
4. Push the vegetables to one side of the skillet and pour the lightly beaten eggs into the other side. Scramble the eggs until they are cooked through, then mix them with the vegetables.
5. Add the cooked white rice and cooked chicken back to the skillet, along with the soy sauce and oyster sauce (if using). Stir everything together until well combined.
6. Cook the fried rice for an additional 2-3 minutes, stirring frequently, until it is heated through and the flavors are well blended.
7. Taste the fried rice and adjust the seasoning with additional soy sauce, salt, or pepper if needed.

8. Once done, remove the skillet from the heat and transfer the chicken fried rice to serving plates.
9. Garnish the chicken fried rice with chopped green onions and sesame seeds, if desired.
10. Serve the chicken fried rice hot as a delicious and satisfying meal. Enjoy the flavorful combination of tender chicken, fluffy rice, and colorful vegetables!

Peach Cobbler

Ingredients:

For the peach filling:

- 6 cups sliced fresh or canned peaches (about 6-8 peaches)
- 1/2 cup granulated sugar
- 1 tablespoon lemon juice
- 1 teaspoon vanilla extract
- 1/2 teaspoon ground cinnamon
- 2 tablespoons cornstarch

For the cobbler topping:

- 1 cup all-purpose flour
- 1/2 cup granulated sugar
- 1 teaspoon baking powder
- 1/4 teaspoon salt
- 1/2 cup unsalted butter, melted
- 1/4 cup boiling water

Instructions:

1. Preheat your oven to 375°F (190°C). Grease a 9x13-inch baking dish or similar-sized casserole dish.
2. In a large mixing bowl, combine the sliced peaches, granulated sugar, lemon juice, vanilla extract, ground cinnamon, and cornstarch. Toss until the peaches are well coated with the sugar mixture.
3. Pour the peach mixture into the prepared baking dish, spreading it out evenly.
4. In a separate mixing bowl, combine the all-purpose flour, granulated sugar, baking powder, and salt for the cobbler topping. Stir until well combined.
5. Add the melted butter to the dry ingredients and mix until a thick batter forms.
6. Gradually add the boiling water to the batter, stirring until smooth.
7. Spoon the cobbler topping over the peaches in the baking dish, spreading it out evenly to cover the fruit.
8. Bake the peach cobbler in the preheated oven for 40-45 minutes, or until the topping is golden brown and cooked through.

9. Once done, remove the peach cobbler from the oven and let it cool for a few minutes before serving.
10. Serve the peach cobbler warm, optionally topped with a scoop of vanilla ice cream or a dollop of whipped cream. Enjoy the sweet and comforting flavors of homemade peach cobbler!

Corn Fritters

Ingredients:

- 1 cup all-purpose flour
- 1 teaspoon baking powder
- 1/2 teaspoon salt
- 1/4 teaspoon black pepper
- 2 large eggs
- 1/4 cup milk
- 1 tablespoon melted butter
- 1 cup fresh or frozen corn kernels
- 1/4 cup finely chopped green onions or chives
- Vegetable oil, for frying

Instructions:

1. In a large mixing bowl, whisk together the flour, baking powder, salt, and black pepper.
2. In a separate bowl, beat the eggs, then stir in the milk and melted butter until well combined.
3. Gradually add the wet ingredients to the dry ingredients, stirring until just combined. Do not overmix; a few lumps are okay.
4. Fold in the corn kernels and chopped green onions or chives until evenly distributed throughout the batter.
5. Heat vegetable oil in a large skillet over medium-high heat until it reaches 350°F (175°C).
6. Once the oil is hot, drop spoonfuls of the batter into the skillet, using about 2 tablespoons of batter for each fritter. Use the back of the spoon to gently flatten the batter into rounds.
7. Fry the corn fritters for 2-3 minutes on each side, or until they are golden brown and crispy.
8. Use a slotted spoon to transfer the cooked fritters to a plate lined with paper towels to drain any excess oil.
9. Repeat the frying process with the remaining batter, making sure not to overcrowd the skillet.

10. Serve the corn fritters hot as a delicious appetizer or side dish. Enjoy their crispy exterior and tender, flavorful interior! Optional: Serve with a dipping sauce like sriracha mayo or sweet chili sauce for extra flavor.

Baked Macaroni and Cheese

Ingredients:

- 8 ounces elbow macaroni (or any pasta shape you prefer)
- 2 tablespoons unsalted butter
- 2 tablespoons all-purpose flour
- 2 cups milk (whole milk works best)
- 2 cups shredded cheese (such as cheddar, Monterey Jack, or a combination)
- 1/2 teaspoon salt, or to taste
- 1/4 teaspoon black pepper, or to taste
- 1/4 teaspoon paprika (optional, for added flavor)
- 1/4 cup breadcrumbs (optional, for topping)

Instructions:

1. Preheat your oven to 350°F (175°C). Grease a 9x13-inch baking dish or similar-sized casserole dish.
2. Cook the elbow macaroni according to the package instructions until al dente. Drain the cooked pasta and set it aside.
3. In a large saucepan or skillet, melt the butter over medium heat. Once melted, whisk in the all-purpose flour to create a roux. Cook the roux, stirring constantly, for 1-2 minutes to remove the raw flour taste.
4. Gradually pour the milk into the saucepan, whisking continuously to prevent lumps from forming. Cook the mixture, stirring frequently, until it thickens slightly and comes to a gentle simmer, about 5-7 minutes.
5. Reduce the heat to low and gradually stir in the shredded cheese, a handful at a time, until it is fully melted and the sauce is smooth and creamy.
6. Season the cheese sauce with salt, black pepper, and paprika to taste. Adjust the seasoning as needed.
7. Add the cooked elbow macaroni to the cheese sauce, stirring until the pasta is evenly coated.
8. Transfer the macaroni and cheese mixture to the prepared baking dish, spreading it out evenly.
9. If desired, sprinkle breadcrumbs evenly over the top of the macaroni and cheese for a crispy topping.
10. Bake the macaroni and cheese in the preheated oven for 20-25 minutes, or until the top is golden brown and the edges are bubbly.

11. Once done, remove the baked macaroni and cheese from the oven and let it cool for a few minutes before serving.
12. Serve the baked macaroni and cheese hot as a comforting and satisfying dish. Enjoy the creamy, cheesy goodness!

Coleslaw

Ingredients:

For the coleslaw:

- 1 small head of cabbage (about 1 1/2 pounds), finely shredded
- 2 large carrots, grated
- 1/2 cup mayonnaise
- 2 tablespoons apple cider vinegar
- 1 tablespoon Dijon mustard
- 2 tablespoons granulated sugar
- 1/2 teaspoon salt
- 1/4 teaspoon black pepper

Instructions:

1. In a large mixing bowl, combine the finely shredded cabbage and grated carrots. Toss them together until well mixed.
2. In a separate smaller bowl, whisk together the mayonnaise, apple cider vinegar, Dijon mustard, granulated sugar, salt, and black pepper until smooth and well combined.
3. Pour the dressing over the cabbage and carrot mixture. Toss everything together until the vegetables are evenly coated with the dressing.
4. Cover the bowl with plastic wrap or a lid and refrigerate the coleslaw for at least 1 hour before serving. This allows the flavors to meld together and the coleslaw to chill.
5. Before serving, give the coleslaw a good stir to recombine the dressing with the vegetables.
6. Serve the coleslaw cold as a refreshing side dish with barbecue, sandwiches, fried chicken, or any other favorite meal.
7. Enjoy the crunchy, creamy goodness of homemade coleslaw! You can also customize your coleslaw by adding ingredients like chopped apples, raisins, or chopped nuts for extra flavor and texture.

Lemon Bars

Ingredients:

For the crust:

- 1 cup all-purpose flour
- 1/4 cup granulated sugar
- 1/2 cup unsalted butter, softened

For the lemon filling:

- 4 large eggs
- 1 1/2 cups granulated sugar
- 1/3 cup fresh lemon juice (about 2-3 lemons)
- 2 tablespoons lemon zest (from about 2 lemons)
- 1/4 cup all-purpose flour
- Powdered sugar, for dusting

Instructions:

1. Preheat your oven to 350°F (175°C). Grease a 9x13-inch baking dish or line it with parchment paper, leaving some overhang on the sides for easy removal.
2. In a mixing bowl, combine the flour, granulated sugar, and softened butter for the crust. Mix until the ingredients come together and form a crumbly dough.
3. Press the dough evenly into the bottom of the prepared baking dish. Use your fingers or the back of a spoon to press the dough firmly into the pan.
4. Bake the crust in the preheated oven for 15-20 minutes, or until it is lightly golden brown around the edges. Remove the crust from the oven and set it aside to cool slightly.
5. While the crust is cooling, prepare the lemon filling. In a separate mixing bowl, whisk together the eggs, granulated sugar, lemon juice, lemon zest, and flour until smooth and well combined.
6. Pour the lemon filling over the partially baked crust, spreading it out evenly.
7. Return the baking dish to the oven and bake for an additional 20-25 minutes, or until the filling is set and the edges are lightly golden brown.
8. Once done, remove the lemon bars from the oven and let them cool completely in the baking dish.
9. Once cooled, dust the top of the lemon bars with powdered sugar.

10. Use the parchment paper overhang to lift the cooled lemon bars out of the baking dish. Place them on a cutting board and slice them into squares or bars.
11. Serve the lemon bars at room temperature and enjoy their bright, tangy flavor!
12. Store any leftover lemon bars in an airtight container in the refrigerator for up to 3-4 days.

Strawberry Jam

Ingredients:

- 2 pounds fresh strawberries, washed, hulled, and chopped
- 2 cups granulated sugar
- 2 tablespoons freshly squeezed lemon juice

Instructions:

1. Place the chopped strawberries in a large, heavy-bottomed pot or saucepan. Mash the strawberries with a potato masher or fork to your desired consistency (some people prefer chunky jam, while others prefer smoother jam).
2. Stir in the granulated sugar and lemon juice until well combined. Let the mixture sit for about 10-15 minutes to allow the sugar to dissolve and the flavors to meld.
3. Place the pot over medium-high heat and bring the strawberry mixture to a boil, stirring frequently to prevent sticking and burning.
4. Once the mixture reaches a boil, reduce the heat to medium-low and let it simmer gently, stirring occasionally, for about 30-40 minutes, or until the jam has thickened to your desired consistency. Keep in mind that the jam will continue to thicken as it cools.
5. While the jam is cooking, prepare your canning jars and lids by sterilizing them in boiling water for about 10 minutes.
6. Once the jam has reached your desired consistency, remove the pot from the heat and carefully ladle the hot jam into the sterilized jars, leaving about 1/4 inch of space at the top of each jar.
7. Wipe the rims of the jars with a clean, damp cloth to remove any spills or residue. Place the lids on the jars and screw on the bands until they are fingertip-tight.
8. Process the filled jars in a boiling water bath for 10 minutes to ensure proper sealing and preservation.
9. After processing, carefully remove the jars from the water bath and let them cool completely at room temperature. As they cool, you should hear the satisfying "pop" sound of the lids sealing.
10. Once cooled, store the sealed jars of strawberry jam in a cool, dark place for long-term storage. Any jars that didn't seal properly should be refrigerated and used within a few weeks.
11. Enjoy your homemade strawberry jam on toast, biscuits, scones, or as a delicious topping for yogurt or ice cream!

BBQ Ribs

Ingredients:

For the ribs:

- 2 racks of baby back ribs or St. Louis-style ribs
- Salt and black pepper, to taste
- Your favorite BBQ rub or seasoning blend (optional)

For the BBQ sauce:

- 1 cup ketchup
- 1/4 cup apple cider vinegar
- 1/4 cup brown sugar
- 2 tablespoons Worcestershire sauce
- 1 tablespoon Dijon mustard
- 1 tablespoon smoked paprika
- 1 teaspoon garlic powder
- 1 teaspoon onion powder
- Salt and black pepper, to taste

Instructions:

1. Preheat your grill to medium heat (about 275-300°F/135-150°C) for indirect grilling.
2. Prepare the ribs by removing the membrane from the back of the ribs, if present. Season both sides of the ribs generously with salt, black pepper, and your favorite BBQ rub or seasoning blend, if using. Let the ribs sit at room temperature for about 30 minutes while you prepare the BBQ sauce.
3. In a small saucepan, combine all the ingredients for the BBQ sauce. Bring the mixture to a simmer over medium heat, then reduce the heat to low and let it cook for about 10-15 minutes, stirring occasionally, until the sauce thickens slightly. Taste and adjust the seasoning as needed.
4. Place the seasoned ribs on the grill, meat side up, over indirect heat. Close the lid and let the ribs cook for about 1 1/2 to 2 hours, or until they are tender and

cooked through. If using a charcoal grill, you may need to add more charcoal or adjust the vents to maintain a consistent temperature.
5. About 30 minutes before the ribs are done cooking, start basting them with the BBQ sauce, brushing it on generously every 10 minutes or so.
6. Once the ribs are tender and have reached your desired level of doneness, remove them from the grill and let them rest for a few minutes before slicing.
7. Serve the BBQ ribs hot, sliced between the bones, and accompanied by any remaining BBQ sauce on the side. Enjoy the smoky, flavorful goodness of homemade BBQ ribs!

Feel free to adjust the cooking time and temperature based on your grill setup and personal preferences. You can also finish the ribs under a broiler or on a hot grill for a few minutes to caramelize the BBQ sauce if desired.

Farmhouse Omelette

Ingredients:

- 4 large eggs
- 2 tablespoons milk or cream
- Salt and pepper, to taste
- 1 tablespoon unsalted butter
- 1/4 cup diced onion
- 1/4 cup diced bell pepper
- 1/4 cup diced cooked ham or bacon
- 1/4 cup diced cooked potatoes
- 1/4 cup shredded cheddar cheese
- Chopped fresh herbs (such as parsley or chives) for garnish (optional)

Instructions:

1. In a mixing bowl, whisk together the eggs, milk or cream, salt, and pepper until well combined. Set aside.
2. Heat the butter in a non-stick skillet over medium heat until melted and foamy.
3. Add the diced onion and bell pepper to the skillet and cook, stirring occasionally, until they are softened and starting to brown, about 3-4 minutes.
4. Add the diced ham or bacon and cooked potatoes to the skillet, stirring to combine with the onions and peppers. Cook for an additional 2-3 minutes, or until the ingredients are heated through.
5. Pour the whisked egg mixture into the skillet, making sure it evenly covers the ingredients.
6. Cook the omelette over medium heat, lifting the edges with a spatula and tilting the skillet to allow the uncooked egg mixture to flow underneath. Continue cooking until the bottom is set and the top is mostly set but still slightly runny.
7. Sprinkle the shredded cheddar cheese evenly over one half of the omelette.
8. Carefully fold the other half of the omelette over the cheese to create a half-moon shape.
9. Cook the omelette for an additional 1-2 minutes, or until the cheese is melted and the omelette is cooked through to your liking.
10. Slide the omelette onto a serving plate and garnish with chopped fresh herbs, if desired.

11. Serve the Farmhouse Omelette hot, accompanied by toast, biscuits, or your favorite breakfast sides. Enjoy the hearty and flavorful combination of eggs, vegetables, meat, and cheese!

Chocolate Chip Cookies

Ingredients:

- 1 cup (2 sticks) unsalted butter, softened
- 3/4 cup granulated sugar
- 3/4 cup packed brown sugar
- 2 large eggs
- 1 teaspoon vanilla extract
- 2 1/4 cups all-purpose flour
- 1 teaspoon baking soda
- 1/2 teaspoon salt
- 2 cups semisweet chocolate chips

Instructions:

1. Preheat your oven to 375°F (190°C). Line baking sheets with parchment paper or lightly grease them.
2. In a large mixing bowl, cream together the softened butter, granulated sugar, and brown sugar until light and fluffy.
3. Beat in the eggs, one at a time, until well combined. Stir in the vanilla extract.
4. In a separate bowl, whisk together the all-purpose flour, baking soda, and salt.
5. Gradually add the dry ingredients to the wet ingredients, mixing until a smooth dough forms.
6. Stir in the semisweet chocolate chips until they are evenly distributed throughout the dough.
7. Drop rounded tablespoons of dough onto the prepared baking sheets, spacing them about 2 inches apart.
8. Bake the cookies in the preheated oven for 8-10 minutes, or until the edges are golden brown and the centers are set.
9. Remove the cookies from the oven and let them cool on the baking sheets for a few minutes before transferring them to wire racks to cool completely.
10. Once cooled, store the chocolate chip cookies in an airtight container at room temperature for up to 5 days.
11. Enjoy the classic homemade goodness of chocolate chip cookies with a glass of milk or your favorite hot beverage!

Feel free to customize your chocolate chip cookies by adding nuts, dried fruits, or different types of chocolate chips, or by chilling the dough before baking for thicker cookies.

Farmhouse Breakfast Hash

Ingredients:

- 4 slices bacon, chopped
- 1 small onion, diced
- 2 cloves garlic, minced
- 2 medium potatoes, peeled and diced
- 1 bell pepper, diced
- 1 cup diced cooked ham or sausage
- Salt and pepper, to taste
- 1 teaspoon paprika
- 1/2 teaspoon dried thyme
- 1/2 teaspoon dried rosemary
- 4 large eggs
- Chopped fresh parsley or green onions, for garnish (optional)

Instructions:

1. In a large skillet, cook the chopped bacon over medium heat until crisp. Remove the bacon from the skillet and drain it on paper towels, leaving the bacon fat in the skillet.
2. Add the diced onion to the skillet with the bacon fat and cook over medium heat until softened, about 3-4 minutes. Add the minced garlic and cook for an additional 1 minute, stirring frequently.
3. Add the diced potatoes to the skillet and cook, stirring occasionally, until they are golden brown and crispy on the outside and tender on the inside, about 10-12 minutes.
4. Stir in the diced bell pepper and cooked ham or sausage. Cook for an additional 3-4 minutes, or until the bell pepper is softened and the meat is heated through.
5. Season the hash with salt, pepper, paprika, dried thyme, and dried rosemary, adjusting the seasoning to taste.
6. Create 4 wells in the hash mixture with the back of a spoon. Crack one egg into each well.
7. Cover the skillet with a lid and cook the eggs over medium-low heat until they are cooked to your desired doneness, about 5-7 minutes for runny yolks or longer for firmer yolks.

8. Once the eggs are cooked, sprinkle the crispy bacon pieces over the top of the hash.
9. Garnish the farmhouse breakfast hash with chopped fresh parsley or green onions, if desired.
10. Serve the farmhouse breakfast hash hot, straight from the skillet, and enjoy the hearty and flavorful combination of potatoes, vegetables, meat, and eggs!

Feel free to customize your farmhouse breakfast hash by adding other ingredients like diced tomatoes, shredded cheese, or cooked beans.

www.ingramcontent.com/pod-product-compliance
Lightning Source LLC
LaVergne TN
LVHW061945070526
838199LV00060B/3982